The Superheroes Of The Cross

PAULA MATTHEWS

Spirit & Life
Publications[SM]

The Superheroes Of The Cross

Copyright ©2011 Paula Matthews

Cover: Paula Matthews

Unless otherwise noted, scripture quotations are from
The Holy Bible: Authorized King James Version,
©2003 Thomas Nelson, Inc.

Published by
Spirit & Life Publications^{SM}
Los Angeles

Printed in the United States
ISBN: 978-0-9729130-6-5

CONTENTS

INTRODUCTION

THE SUPERHERO ANALOGY

A SUPERHERO SPEAKS

CONCLUSION

MORE FROM THE AUTHOR

ENDNOTES

IF ANY MAN BE
IN CHRIST
HE IS A
NEW CREATURE
(Unprecedented Species of Mankind)

II Corinthians 5:17

IN JESUS . . .
THE ONLY THING THAT COUNTS
IS THE NEW CREATION
Galatians 6:15

INTRODUCTION

Life Beyond The Cross; The Mystery Revealed

Like most baby-boomers, I grew up in the generation of television superheroes. These programs had such an impact, that every little kid on my block knew that they too could be a superhero. It didn't take much to convince children, because deep within us was a yearning for greatness; a longing to do supernatural acts in order to save the world. It was almost instinctive. Then I recall spending time with my great-grand mother. She lived in the country and didn't have television, so in the evening she would pull out her Bible and read some of the most amazing stories of children and ordinary people who were superheroes for God. Listening to those Bible stories kept me and my siblings on the edge of our seats. Granny made those stories seem more real than the stories we saw on television. I remember her telling us that these were not made up characters like on TV. These were real people who believed God could do the impossible, and because they believed, God did mighty works through their lives. But how could this be?

How could a young boy like David kill a giant with a sling slot and then later become a king?[i] How could Daniel as a boy survive in a lion's den and not be killed?[ii] Shadrach, Meshach and Abednego were three boys thrown into a fiery furnace and they were not burned.[iii] Not a hair singed and they didn't even smell like smoke. From Genesis to Revelation, the Bible is filled with stories of man's battle of good versus evil; and within every battle a hero arose to the occasion and changed the world. Miracles began to happen. Dead people were brought back to life. People were healed from diseases such as leprosy and epilepsy.[iv]

The blind could see and the lame could walk.[v] And during time of lack, God brought food and money from out of nowhere.[vi] A man changed times and seasons by causing a draught and then three years later he causes rain to come upon the land.[vii] Another man caused the sun to stand still, and the moon to stop until he defeated all the enemies of God.[viii] People slew armies of their enemies just by singing praises to God. Others took down fortified cities by walking around the city walls, and as they shouted the walls fell down.[ix] These stories were vastly different from what I experienced in my Midwestern Baptist church. There were no miracles. No one was ever healed; many were bound by lust and demons; but we were saved and planned on going to heaven when we died. Even as a child, something didn't make sense to me. "What good is having Jesus in my heart, if he could not help me today?" I kept looking in the Bible and noticed that when people encountered Jesus, their lives were radically changed. They didn't have to wait to get to heaven in order have their lives changed. Jesus answered them immediately and they received what they needed. He even asked what they wanted him to do for them. He was always willing and ready to help people in that same moment. This is the Jesus I sought after. It was my desire to prove that the Bible stories were real.

When I became an adult, the Spirit of God explained to me, that before Jesus came to earth, men could only perform miracles, as His Spirit would come upon men for a specific task. A Holy God could not dwell where there was sin, so he sent Jesus to earth, not only to deal with the sin issue, but also to show men how to live on earth. Jesus came preaching the Kingdom of God and demonstrating its power. He told his followers that the Holy Spirit would dwell within them, to be a teacher, a guide and a comforter in this earth. After his resurrection he told his disciples that *when they received the Holy Spirit, they would receive power*. It was the Holy Spirit that led Jesus while he lived upon the earth. It was also the Holy Spirit that showed Jesus what God the Father was saying and doing in heaven. He relayed information and instructions from God in heaven and delivered them directly to Jesus' spirit. It was the Holy Spirit that raised Jesus from the dead. This power is now made available to men on earth so that they can resurrect the situations of their lives to the glory of God the father. All who receive Jesus are given the authority to live like sons of God in the earth.

God is looking for sons who will imitate him and release God's great mysteries in the earth. For every problem that we face in this life, from financial recession, to lack of natural resources, to undiscovered cures and industrial inventions, God has a solution that he is eager to share with his sons. On our own, we cannot produce anything that brings optimum satisfaction. Without the infinite wisdom of God, and the Holy Spirit, men are limited. Our world is experiencing rampant system failures because these systems were built upon the wisdom and ingenuity of human beings. As Creator, God is all knowing. Men are limited by their education and human wisdom; therefore everything they create is also limited and destined to fail. God is infinite in his wisdom, but he will generously impart that wisdom to anyone who asks of him. God alone knows how to repair and replenish any and all systems in this world. All it takes, is for someone with a Kingdom connection to ask in prayer and God will relay the appropriate instructions back to earth. This is life beyond the cross. It's about more than making Jesus our personal Lord and Savior. This is about changing our lives, in an effort to change the world around us; making life better for all mankind.

Imagine a human being possessing the power to rescue a family, a community or a nation from destruction. How about rescuing the world? Believe or not, this supernatural power is lying dormant within us and all it would take to resurrect this power is reconnecting to God (the Source), thereby activating the superhero within us to overcome any issue we could ever encounter in this life.

The Spiritual Evolution Of One New Man

The shortest distance between two points is a straight line. The explanation of God's plan for man on earth can also be described in a straight line manner. The initial or beginning point is Adam. The end point is Jesus; who is also called the last Adam. It is the significance of these two points in human history that God has prescribed a line demarcating the sole purpose of all humanity from Genesis to Revelation. It's a purpose not based on law, but on love. It's not about church or religion it's about relationship and the family of God. It's about an inheritance God desires to give to those who will obey him under the plan, purpose and government of the Kingdom of God. There have been many messengers, howbeit; the message has been muddled due to human misunderstanding and misinterpretation. We thought it was about religion and which religion was the right path to God; but it's much more than that. It's about returning to God and claiming an inheritance of wealth, power and dominion to replenish, repair and restore this earth and its inhabitants to God's original plan.

Adam was created as the first of a new breed of creation made in the image and likeness of God, operating in the character and manner of God; a species that would take dominion and distribute the plan and wealth of heaven throughout the earth. Every nation, race and tongue, was to flow out of Adam's loins in righteousness. The would live under the blessing until they filled the whole earth with the glory of God, but went terribly wrong. Adam sinned, thereby cursing all human kind to live a life of apart from God in pain, suffering, lack and death. Adam's sin left men on earth with a spiritual void. Men created religion in an attempt to fill that void and create their own paths back to

God. In the Garden of Eden there was no need for church or religion because God communed directly with his son Adam. There was no barrier between them. This was God's grand design for man. This was God's earthly family. It was never suppose to change. God would commune with his sons on earth. They were to be humans living on earth dominating and ruling like their father in heaven; operating under the leadership and authority of heaven. Adam's sin changed everything. It put a wide chasm between God and his earthly creation.

Today, people don't usually seek God until tragedy comes. But God is always looking for us.[x] He proved it when he sent Jesus to earth in search of his lost love . . . ADAM (Mankind). Jesus came to show us the way back to God. Jesus also made the bold claim that he was *the only way* to God.[xi] This statement offended the Jews in Jesus' day and it still offends people today; but God shared something with me that made it perfectly clear. Remember that the key idea in God's plan is about qualifying people for an inheritance; the inheritance that Adam lost. Jesus said that the way was narrow, and few would even find it.[xii] But think about it; you can't even receive an earthly inheritance without satisfying a narrow set of preliminary criteria. How much more specific should they be when God is talking about giving us an inheritance that includes world domination, and all the power and wealth of heaven that is to be distributed upon the earth?

Jesus is God's only designated path to the restoration of this inheritance. Everyone who receives Jesus, regardless of their nation, race or tongue, becomes a new creation; a new species of human being that is uniquely reconnected

to God by His Spirit. Again, it's not about religion, or de-
nomination. It is about restoring God's family on earth. It
is about knowing and relating to God as a son; just like
Jesus related to God.

In God's Kingdom men are no longer divided by religion
such as Jew or Gentile. Neither are we divided as Slave or
Free, Male or Female, Black, White, Brown, Yellow or Red
Man; in God's Kingdom we are ONE NEW MAN, One New
Adam, the BODY OF CHRIST, united as One Body and
One Spirit, in communion under one Lord, one faith, One
baptism; One God and Father of all . . . One family of God
united both in heaven and in earth made up of people from
every nation, tribe and tongue, subject to the peace and
blessings of God unto ETERNAL LIFE FOREVER. This is
the message of the Gospel of the Kingdom of God.

Jesus died so that we (the new creation/new man) should
no longer live for ourselves, but for him who died and was
raised from the dead for us. Now, anyone who is willing
to totally surrender his life can take on the life of a Son
of God; to be led by the Spirit of God doing mighty acts of
God in defense of the suffering masses; to comfort all who
mourn by giving them the Good News of God's Kingdom.
This is the superhero's call in the Kingdom.

THE SUPERHERO
ANALOGY

The Superhero's Creed

THE SPIRIT OF THE LORD IS UPON ME BECAUSE:

He Has Anointed Me
To Preach The Gospel
To The Poor

He Has Sent Me
<u>To Heal</u>
The Brokenhearted

<u>To Preach</u>
Deliverance To The Captives
And Recovery Of Sight To The Blind,

<u>To Set At Liberty</u>
Those Who Are Bruised

<u>To Proclaim</u>
The Acceptable Year Of The Lord
(The Day Of God's Vengeance
To Comfort All Who Mourn)

Luke 4:18-19; Isaiah 61:1-2

The Sons Of God Are The Ultimate Superheroes

A superhero is one possessing extraordinary powers or skills by virtue of a divine or supernatural source; one whose mission is to utilize his or her true-to-life superpowers to protect humanity from the evil forces in the universe. If you think that superheroes are just fictional characters, think again. In this chapter we will prove that the Sons of God are superheroes. They are the ultimate superheroes of this world!

While the word *superhero* does not literally appear in the Bible, there is a vast amount of scripture that shows how God has chosen his sons to be heaven's superintendents and defenders of this earth. This is the same job he gave Adam at creation. He was told to tend and protect the Garden of Eden.[xiii] In addition to caring for the land, God has promised to give his sons the nations of the world as an inheritance.[xiv] The sons of God are called to be kings and priests unto God.[xv] Since God's Kingdom is a spiritual one, it is expected that the sons of God would rule on earth in preparing the people for Jesus' ultimate rule in his millennial reign in the near future. Until that time, those who receive an abundance of God's grace (favor) and his gift of righteousness (through salvation), will be expected to reign in this life through Jesus Christ. In the future, they will also reign with Jesus upon the earth for one thousand years.

The sons of God are given a portion of their inheritance through the Holy Spirit. It is the Holy Spirit who supernaturally empowers men to do impossible feats in the earth.[xvi] Why does God do this for humans? Because he loves us, and he wants to give us the best life ever. God loves us just like he loves Jesus; therefore as Jesus is (in heaven) so are we in this world.[xvii]Jesus sits at the right hand of God's throne, and as sons, we are seated together with Jesus; and have been given all the spiritual blessings in heaven.[xviii] As sons, we are joint heirs with Jesus of God's entire kingdom; that includes empowerment and blessings laid up in heaven and upon the earth.

Some might wonder. If God is in heaven, how is it possible for him to conceive and bear children on this earth? At creation, God created his first born son Adam from the dust of the ground and breathed life into his being. The glory of God was also placed inside of man. When Adam sinned, the glory left man, and it left the earth. God had to find a way to restore mankind to his former glory. Jesus, who is called the Last Adam, was born of a human vessel. God found a virgin named Mary, and impregnated her by the Holy Spirit; resulting in a supernatural conception, but a natural birth. In order to create a new humanity, God would have find a way to place his glory inside of men. He would utilize the same Holy Spirit that conceived Jesus into the womb of Mary. Men would have to be born again of the Spirit. This is a mystery of salvation. When one receives Jesus, they are also receiving the Holy Spirit which houses the entire Kingdom in all of It's glory. None of this would have been possible if Jesus has not died and resurrected. It was not until after the resurrection that the same Holy Spirit that raised Jesus from the dead, became available to born again men. God chose to utilize the law of sowing and reaping. He sowed (planted) his son Jesus in the earth in order to reap a harvest of sons in the earth. So, when Jesus was crucified and buried in the ground, he was as a seed that germinated in the ground. He arose from the grave and the evidence of his resurrection caused many to desire to become sons as well. This supernatural harvesting of sons will continue until Jesus returns to earth to gather his earthly family and take them to heaven. So who exactly are these Sons of God? These are the men and women who are born of God. Anyone who receives Jesus as Lord of their life has the potential to become a son of God. Therefore, the first step in becoming a son is to be born again.[xix]

Jesus was born fully human and fully divine; but he walked the earth as a human who was filled and guided by the Spirit of God. This was his connection to his father in heaven. Mary conceived Jesus after the angel spoke the word, it was the Holy Spirit that carried out that word. Likewise, we were born again after hearing the word about the Kingdom and the power of the resurrection. It is also the Holy Spirit carries out that word in our lives.

When God speaks and we believe what we hear; this is called faith. The Spirit of God always responds to our faith. Whatever that faith produces, is a divine nature. Yes, Jesus had a divine nature and when we believed in him, we became partakers of that divine nature which begins to manifest in our lives through the Holy Spirit.[xx] The greatest part of that divine nature is love. A personal revelation of God's love alone, will make you feel like a superhero. When you get a glimpse of God's love, you will begin to see as he sees and feel as he feels about people and situations in this earth. Compassion comes over you, and your spirit will approach God for a solution. Before you know it, you are equipped and empowered with a solution. You may even carry out the will of God before your mind and body can figure out what has happened. If your spirit is willing, and it comes into agreement with the Spirit of God, then all things will be possible for you. Our love towards God is demonstrated when we keep his commandments. God also expects us to show unconditional love for one another. We are to show compassion by putting another's needs above our selfish desires. Love reveals suffering to you, but compassion compels us to action. This is part of God's purpose for his sons. In fact, Psalm 2:8 says that if we ask of God, he will give us the nations for our inheritance and the entire earth for our possession.

The earth needs superheroes. No longer will there be one or two notable mighty men of valor. God is creating a mighty army of powerful men and women to reach the lost and hurting masses in the nations of the world. An effective superhero must be able to rise above the crowd to hear the cries of the suffering. God is the champion of the downtrodden, the hurting masses who have been left destitute by this world. God always restores a thing to the original specifications that he designed from the foundation of the world. To restore people back to the design God had for Adam; is a miracle!

Poverty, lack, sickness and disease are evidence of Adam's curse in the earth. The sons of God are supernaturally empowered (anointed) to eradicate the curse. Jesus, along with the father, and the Holy Spirit, did supernatural deeds in the earth in the past. What a terrific trio of superheroes! Today, Jesus said that those who believe and follow after him would do even greater works in the earth (John 14:12)! God saved the best for last. God's best plan for your life is greater than anything you could imagine on your own. Let's continue by showing how you can become a Superhero Of The Cross.

He has delivered us from
The power of darkness and translated us into
The Kingdom of His Dear Son
Colossians 1:13

TRANSFORMATION

CHANGE
BEGINS
HERE

<----

"Except a man be
Born Again,
He cannot see
The Kingdom of God."
JOHN 3:3

The Cross Is Our Transformation Phone Booth

Every comic book superhero has a mode and a locale where they transformed from the human to the "super" human form. The Kingdom of God holds the mystery of God's transformation plan for your life. God has a time and purpose for every human who lives upon the earth. It is a plan for good and not evil; a plan that offers a good future and hope (Jeremiah 29:11). God has also placed within the hearts of every human a yearning to know and fulfill his or her purpose in the world. But, that yearning cannot be filled by human efforts, but by God alone (Ecclesiastes 3:11).

The purpose for every human is revealed by the Spirit of God. The human eye has not seen, nor has ear, heard, neither has it entered into the hearts of man what God has planned for those who love him. God reveals it by His Spirit (I Corinthians 2:9-11). You must be plugged-in to God's Spirit to receive from God's Kingdom. This plug-in is freely given to those who receive Jesus as Lord. You must have a heart willing and ready to receive from God. Your heart is the receiver of information from God. God is the source. The Holy Spirit relays information from heaven, but Jesus is the Way to the source (God). Some will say that there are many ways to God. It's because they don't know God's original plan for mankind and how Adam disconnected us from that plan. His sin resulted in the chasm between God and man. God sent Jesus (the embodiment of God) to repair that chasm. It is because of the Blood of Jesus that sin was paid for, and the connection to God is restored. We don't have to find a way to God. The father came down from heaven and made a way for us. He decreed that Jesus was the only way back to God (John 14:6). Through His Blood Jesus received power, riches, wisdom, strength, honor, glory and blessing for us (Revelation 5:12). He received everything on our behalf. To receive these things, one must be born again. *Unless a man is born again, he cannot perceive the things of the Kingdom of God* (John 3:3). Perception is done in the heart. Sin blinds the heart of God's will for their lives. To see God, the heart must be purified. The process begins at the cross of Jesus Christ.

Adam was God's first son in this earth. He was Blessed to be fruitful and multiply every righteous and good thing heaven had placed within the earth. Through Adam's loins would come every person into this earth. According to God's original plan, every man would have been born under the Blessing and the curse. Every man would have lived in an Eden of his own; in a pleasant place where there was only good and no evil. BUT, Adam had another plan that resulted in sin. After Adam sinned, all humans were doomed to born into sin. The penalty for sin is death, which means eternal separation from God and all the goodness he desires for our lives. It was not God's desire that men die. God wants all men to be saved from death, and made knowledgeable of the truth of his love for us (I Timothy 2:4). Truth came in the form of Jesus Christ, the son of God. Jesus shed his blood and died on the cross to pay the penalty for our sins, so we could be restored to our wealthy place in God.

The gospel of God's Kingdom is that the Blessing has been restored to mankind. We don't have to die any more. We don't have to live with demons, or sickness or lack any more. If God would raise Jesus out of the grave, then God could raise us up out of everything evil that has kept us bound in this earth. This is the kind of faith one needs to be saved from spiritual death (separation) from God. Salvation requires that one surrenders to God. One must let go of his or her past, and desires for this life, in order to take hold of God's future greatness and his wonderful desires for our lives. This is a heart transformation; an exchange of our life for one in God's Kingdom of power and glory.

All one needs to do is believe. If you confess with your mouth the desire to make Jesus Lord of your life, and believe in your heart that God raised Jesus from the dead, you will be saved (Roman 10:9). The transformation begins immediately. The Holy Spirit comes to live in your heart. He deposits the love of God within you. The Holy Spirit places God's Kingdom, his righteousness, love, provision and power within you. It is in this transformation that Superheroes Of The Cross are made. One now has the capacity to think like God; act like God; and speak like God in the earth. This is the original plan for mankind on earth. This is how Adam operated before he sinned. This is how Jesus operated when he walked the earth. Jesus said and did only what God the father told him to say and do. Jesus walked this earth like God, because he was God.

That same GOD POWER resides within every one who is saved. It is given for the purpose of saving the earth and it inhabitants from destruction and restoring it all back to God. This is a SUPERHERO PURPOSE for a God-man; a supernaturally powered human, born of God's spirit as a son of God, and god and ruler over the things of this earth. We are commanded to rule on earth as it is in heaven (Matthew 6:10). To do so, one's heart and mind must be continually transformed as we increase in the knowledge of God's word.

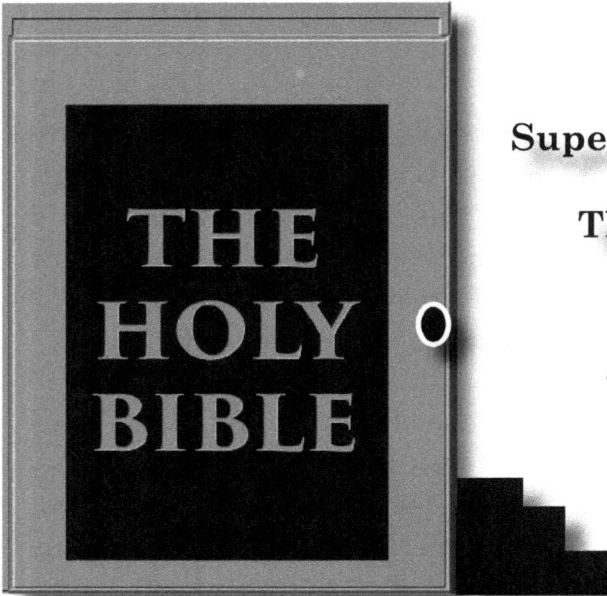

The Bible: Supernatural Portal To The Kingdom Of God

"I Am The Door: by me
If any man enter in,
He shall be saved,
And shall go in and out,
And find pasture."
JOHN 10:9

Once a person has activated his connection with God by receiving Jesus Christ as Savior and Lord, it is very important that he or she immediately starts reading the Bible. The Bible is called the Living Word of God. It is *The Instruction Book* for every believer, and a *Source Of Spiritual Nutrition* for every Superhero Of The Cross. The Bible feeds the spirit, like food feeds the body. It also heals the body physically and supernaturally. It is a supernatural book that embodies the Spirit of God Himself. When one reads the Bible and acts in obedience to what it says, it is as if God, Himself is operating in the earth.

The Bible is indeed a portal (door) to the supernatural power and purpose of God. The Holy Spirit is the teacher.[xxi] When read along with the guidance of the Holy Spirit, the Bible will create a spiritual opening for one to literally walk through the pages right into the Kingdom of God. Don't be surprised when the letters begin to lift off of the pages and answers your questions or gives you instruction. The Bible is a supernatural book beyond the comprehension of mere men, yet born again men are the only one who can experience this type of spiritual interaction with God and His word. Many people can read the Bible, but when the Bible reads you and speaks to your situation, that is a powerful thing. The word of God is alive and acting, sharper than any two-edged sword. It can divide soul from spirit and joints from the marrow. It is a discerner of the thoughts and intents of the heart.[xxii] It is a mirror into the soul and spirit of man. It shows us who we are now, and what we can become if we turn our whole hearts to God. Therefore the Bible becomes a lamp to our feet and a light to illuminate our path in this life.[xxiii] It is God speaking directly to us, about us.

There is no distinction between God and His word. Therefore when one is born again, it is the seed of God's word that is implanted in the heart of man. It is God inside of man. When the God inside connects with the Bible, a powerful supernatural event happens. We call it a miracle. Men become infused with supernatural power to do the impossible, but it all begins with hearing the word of God, and then acting upon what they have heard. With God, all things are possible. Additionally, all things are possible for those who believe what God is saying in His word. The results of such a communion (partnership) are endless.

God created every living thing with His word. Everything He created has within itself the seed to reproduce itself in this earth. It is the word of God that creates. It is the word of God that sustains all life forms in this earth, even to this day. That is why it is called the *living word*. It is ever increasing and ever ready to produce results that multiply, and replenish what is necessary for life on earth. It is a living organism that produces life. The word of God is seed. The Bible is filled with seed. It is capable of producing whatever God desires for your life. You only need take a specific scripture (seed) and sow it into the ground of your heart. Then watch it grow into full manifestation in your life. God's word never returns to him void. It will always produce what He desires and accomplishes that which He purposes.[xxiv] All God is looking for is a willing partner who is ready to make a difference in the world.

The Bible is our portal (door) to the supernatural Kingdom of God. If God speaks a word to your spirit, it is the same as God himself coming to your assistance. Hearing the voice of God is vital for the superhero. The word that He speaks are spirit and life.[xxv] It has been designed to be the fuel that nourishes and empowers the supernatural part of us. As we feed upon the Word, it will produce within our bodies, minds, spirit and even our physical atmosphere the very thing that is written in the Bible.

The anointing (supernatural power) of God is contained within the Word of God and it is released throughout the atmosphere; revealing open the heavens over your life. God opens up the heavens so that whatever people need will be immediately provided. The windows of heaven open to allow the supernatural power of God to change whatever needs changing in our earth. The superhero sons of God are adept at forging an opening to penetrate heaven where God resides; thereby opening up a portal where heavens resources can flow down into every earthly need.

This book talks about the new creation being a superhero, in actuality it's not about us, it's about a loving God needing his sons to be available vessels of transformation in the earth. It is how God can come down from heaven with all his power and take care of the suffering and hurting masses in this earth.

GOD: The Source Of Our Strength

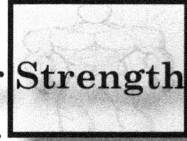

Superheroes of the cross are empowered to be strong in the Lord and the power of his might. The key to a superhero's strength is in knowing that his strength is not from him, but from God (the supernatural source) that is operating within him. It's the God inside of the person that makes him or her a superhero. It's not our power, nor is it our plan and purpose for this earth. The power, the plan and purpose originated from Almighty God. When we agree to take His Spirit, His power and His plan, only then does it become ours, as agents of God in this earth. This is a powerful union of human and the divine.

Comic superheroes are often depicted as humans with divine powers. Some even claim to be offspring of the gods, therefore gods (demigods) themselves. These are all idols. How much more should it be the case with True and Living God and His offspring?[xxvi] Think about it. If your father is One and Only True God, then by birthright the sons and daughters of God would also have a divine nature and would be called gods in their own right. Even so, the Bible calls gods, in whom the word of God has been given.[xxvii] He whom God sends, speaks the words of God.[xxviii] Moses was sent to Pharaoh demanding that he let God's people go free from enslavement. God said that he made Moses a god to Pharaoh.[xxix] Now, imagine, God speaking to sons and daughters and sending them into business, government, or into any sector of our world. As emissaries of God, armed with the word of God, they would be considered gods to those whom they have been sent. In addition, they are the sons of God, doing the will of God, in the power and glory of God in this earth. That is a mighty super heroic task to live up to.

In God's Kingdom superheroes and the situations in which they are made are by God's design. All of our times, seasons and even our places of habitation are predetermined by God.[xxx] In fiction, heroes arise out of some crisis and a need for justice and revenge. In God's Kingdom, superheroes can arise for the same reasons, but rather that taking on the act of revenge on their own; they place the situation in the hands of Almighty God.

A Superhero Of The Cross knows his or her limitations. They will not violate God's word; for in their weakness, they are made strong in the Lord.[xxxi] We have to decrease if God is to increase. When we yield to God's instruction, we will amass an unlimited amount of power from heaven to accomplish God's purpose in that matter. Therefore we are vessels being used by God for a super heroic mission. It is not about us, but about Him, and when we obey Him, it causes the laws of God's Kingdom to supersede every other law in the universe. Now that' real power!

So, whose qualified to receive such power? The answer may surprise you. God doesn't always choose those who we think should be strong heroes. He chooses the weak and makes them strong. He chooses the foolish to confound the wise; those things that seem insignificant and despise he uses. God glories in using those who are of low esteem and making them great so that no man can take the credit.[xxxii] It's God's camouflage effect. Jesus said, that as the wind blows and you don't know which way it comes nor where it is going, so it is with those who are of the spirit. You cannot see them coming nor going because it is the wind of God's Spirit moving them. We see the effects, but how God did it may remain a mystery for all eternity. The job of the

Superhero is to hear the voice of God and obey. He speaks what God speaks, and the father does the work.[xxxiii] He is the Source and the Solution. We are simply obedient servants who God has chosen for such a time as this. Any believer can become a superhero. All it takes is faith. God's superheroes are strengthened in their hearts by the Spirit of God. Therefore we can do all things through Christ (the anointing of God) that strengthens us.[xxxiv]

Each person in God's Kingdom was given the same measure of faith.[xxxv] Every one who receives Jesus as Lord has the authority to walk this earth as a Mighty Son of God empowered by Heaven. All it takes is faith. All things are possible to those who believe.

A little faith can change our world. This kind of faith is not centered in what we can do, but centered in what God can do through us. Our faith is the victory that overcomes the evils of this world. Faith is not just hoping for something good to happen. It is the absolute belief that what God says, will surely come to pass. It is the bold confidence in knowing that God will do what he promised to do!

Satan: The Arch Nemesis

Every superhero has an enemy whose self-proclaimed purpose is to annihilate the mighty man or woman. An arch-enemy is considered one who is recurring nemesis in the life of the hero. It could be a former friend or a determined foe; in any case it is the person who always seems to plague our hero, even though he has no power to overcome that hero. Satan is called a defeated foe. Jesus overcame him after resurrecting from the grave. He took the power of hell and death away from that devil and gave it to the kingdom heroes in this earth.

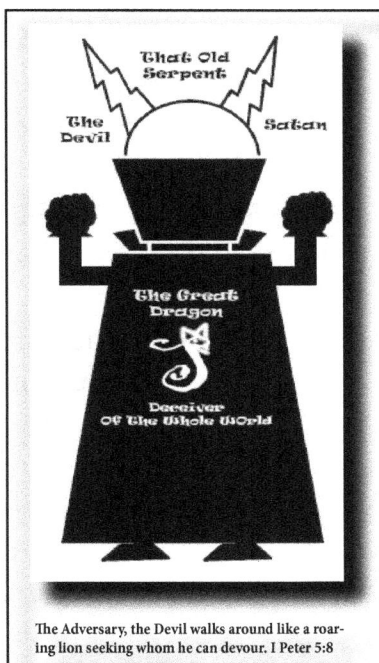

The Adversary, the Devil walks around like a roaring lion seeking whom he can devour. I Peter 5:8

The Bible says that we don't wrestle with people, but with spiritual beings in heavenly places: powers of darkness and principal spiritual rulers of our countries, states and cities. So, our enemies are not people, but the demonic and self serving spirits that motivate and rule these people.[xxxvi]

Most Christians recognize Satan as their arch nemesis, and they are correct. HOWEVER, his methods of operation are custom designed for each specific foe's area of weakness. His tactics appear harmless and unassuming, but his purpose is always to steal, kill and destroy God's sons and daughters in the earth So the minute you first step into the superhero realm, you may get a powerful retaliatory blow from your adversary Satan. Do not fear. The Greater One is in you.

Ask God to reveal the identity of your enemies. Ask that he identify the weapon (scripture) necessary to take them down. Once you have your superhero stride in place, you will find even more opportunities to team up with other heroes on even bigger missions. The more you increase in power, the more the enemy will strike back. Do not fear! You will win every battle, if you don't give up. He has no power over you. The Bible says that the devil walks around like a roaring lion seeking whom he can devour.[xxxvii] He not a lion. He a liar and deceiver. Whatever he tells you, is designed to steal the word of God from you. The word of God is your source of power. If the devil can steal the word, he can steal your promise.

In the comics, superheroes have limitations to his or her power. Almighty God's power is unlimited. The only way a Superhero Of The Cross can limit God's power in this earth, is in their disobedience. We are to become imitators of God in our pursuit of all things, and especially in pursuit of power to change situations on earth. Again, we go after God and his purpose in that situation. Going after power for any other way is unacceptable to God. The devil's kids follow after the power of darkness. They go after witchcraft, voodoo and black arts to gain power. These are outlaws in the realm of the spirit, and are unacceptable to God. They have a form of power, but it is not the True Power that comes only from Almighty God. Therefore, it is imperative that God's sons and daughters follow after their father's instructions to the letter. It insures that they are not walking on the dark side where the power is limited, and in the area where they could get hurt. The Greater On is in them, but they have to be willing to play by the Heaven's rules, and not according to their emotions or how they think.

The devil's kids want power, but God gave power only to His sons and daughters. Everyone in God's Kingdom has been given the authority to tread upon serpents and scorpions and all the power of the enemy, and nothing shall anyway harm them.[xxxviii] This is how God desires to operate through his sons and daughters in the earth It is also important that they know their authority in Jesus Christ. When Jesus resurrected with all the power of heaven and earth, he then gave that power to the believers and told us to go into all the world teaching and multiplying sons in the earth. The moment we think the power is coming from us, we have just stepped out of line with God. The minute we decide to take matters into our own hands rather than waiting on God's instruction, we have just stepped out of His will. The instant we are motivated by hate, pride or revenge and not by the love and compassion of God, we will become the arch enemies of God and the power will become perverted. Rather possessing the power to heal and bless, the "would be" superhero would begin to operate in a curse that would consume him and those in league with him. These superheroes would become powerless, disillusioned and turn into villains. This is how many an arch nemesis began. They did not like the rules and decided to go against God, and make revenge their motive.

One must remember that *All Power In Heaven And In Earth was given to Jesus*, and to those whom are aligned with him and Heaven's purpose for this earth. God put all things under Jesus' authority.[xxxix] All entry into the realm of the spirit outside of Jesus is illegal. God will deal with spiritual outlaws, according to the laws of the Kingdom. No one can escape the judgment of God!

A SUPERHERO SPEAKS

One morning, I heard these words coming out from my spirit.

"As kids, we played, Let's Pretend; what we will have or what we will be. But this life in Christ, we don't have to pretend. We can have what God says, if we don't faint due to pain, sickness and unbelief. If we don't receive, it's because we never really believed."

This Truly Is <u>SUPERHERO</u> Faith!

My story is on the next page!

Caricature By Dani Scott

The Crisis Defined

Many years after my initial quest to find the truth of the Bible, I found myself in an abusive marriage. The miracle of my survival began as I saw the Hand of God protecting me through every attempt on my life. No matter what this man did to me, he could not hurt me. I quickly learned during that time, that the Spirit of God would speak and give me instructions. Whenever I obeyed God's instructions, the devil could not kill me. Obviously I was obedient because I am alive to tell my story.

During this crisis, I recall shaking the Bible in my hands, in the direction of Heaven and asking why my life did not look like what he promised in that book. In fact, I told him that my life was exactly opposite of what the Bible said it should be. I told him that I only wanted to see the truth operating in my life. I was tired of the deception and lies of my marriage, and the oppression and demons it brought into my life. Intermingled in my exclamation was a sincere heart of gratitude that after all my years of ignorance, God saw my pain and intervened on my behalf. I cried out to him and God showed up with a mighty power and released me from a deadly marriage. It was not easy. I had sown some bad seeds by marrying a man God told me to avoid. Even after I obeyed God and left, I endured hardship. The abuse continue. My son was kidnapped. A corrupt judge presided over my divorce case and threatened my life. A contract was put out on my life. My parents endured harassment and threats from court and law enforcement officials. I went through several attorneys. Many were also threatened and fled for their safety. I learned that the man I had married had ties to the mafia. In all these things, I had no fear. Once God told me to leave the marriage it would be only a matter of time before I was truly free.

When my story appeared in newspapers and on television telling about the injustices I endured, women came flocking to my support group, and some even came to my home looking for help. It was though I had struck a chord with so many women. It overwhelmed me. I thought that my situation was both unusual and unique. How wrong I was. People have a belief that what's going on in the home should stay in the home. That makes domestic and child abuse silent killers. People suffer in silence thinking that they are the only ones; that they somehow deserve to be abuse. Even pastors and religious people will send victims of abuse back into that relationship think that they somehow did something wrong that caused the abuse. Not so! God hates abuse. He did not create us to dominate over others. He created us to be a loving and caring family. That was God's original plan for mankind. God, who is Love, created a family He could love; a family who could love like He loves. Family is very important to God. This was the first institution He created in this earth. In God's family, there is no place for abuse, and yet it happens because we are deceived.

There is a deception in abuse that goes through the minds of many victims. You actually believe that no one else knows what it is like to be abused. It's a secret you keep in your house and don't discuss with anyone. Even if you could talk, most people never believe abuse victims until someone ends up severely injured or dead. My case almost had a deadly end. I left the marriage with a gun pointed at my head. During my divorce, the opposing attorney warned that the man I had married had hired a sniper to take me out before I got into the court room. Instead of running scared, I went public. When my story broke, women came to me for help. They came in large numbers, and yet I could not even resolve my own case. I remember crying out to God for help. All these women were coming to me as though I was their savior, yet I had no power to change either their lives or my own. To make matter worse, my ex-husband retaliated against me when the press got involved. He came to the city where we lived and kidnapped my three-year old son. (That was twenty-five years ago. Although God promised that we would see each other again, I have yet to be re-united with my son.)

While going through this trauma, the Spirit of God said that it was the plot of the enemy to tie me up in confusion, and legal nonsense in order to distract me from my purpose in life. Evil came against me because of what God was calling me to do. I didn't know God had a plan for my life, but the devil knew, and he sent his demons and henchmen against me. It was an onslaught of evil sent to make me crack. It did not work. The enemy didn't expect that I would run to God for refuge in my time of trouble. God moved on my behalf supernaturally. I have seen my enemies defeated in an instant. Many lost their minds, some their very lives. The Bible says to touch not my anointed and do my prophets no harm.[xl] God promises to scatter our enemies before our face.[xli] That's exactly what happened for me. His power sustains and rejuvenates me to continue with strength for the ongoing battle. When we hope and rely on God for our victory, he will renew our strength. We will mount up on wings like eagles, we will run and not be weary; we shall walk and shall not faint.[xlii] The Superheroes Of The Cross have extraordinary replenishing power that comes from God alone.

The Transformation

When I told the Lord that I had no power to help the women who were coming to me, He responded by sending me to Los Angeles in search of *His Power*. After arriving to that city, the Spirit of God asked if I was ready to become a son. I said yes, without really knowing what being a son of God really meant. The Lord led me on a twenty-one day fast. It was during this fast that I received *God's Power and His Assignment for my life*. The power of God freaked me out a few times, but I continued to do whatever God said do; go where ever God said go; and say whatever God had me say. When I obeyed God, miracles happened.

The Spirit of God said that He was raising me up to be a **"Giant Slayer in business and industry."** A pastor friend called and prophesied that God was equipping me with **"An anointing (supernatural ability) for technology; for industry and technology of the spiritual realm."** I was anointed with the Holy Ghost and power, sent to industry to heal and do good works.

Every superhero has a specially designed costume that shields them from enemy attacks. As believers our costume is called *spiritual armor*: the belt of truth; the breastplate of righteousness, the gospel of peace as our shoes; the shield of faith and the and the sword of the spirit (Ephesians 6:13-17). But, did you know that God has an armory full or armor and weapons that we have never seen? I was stunned at what I saw in the spirit when the Spirit of God said to me, **"Let me show you, your new armor."** I was heavily clad from head to toe in armor made of thick heavy duty tire tread with long piercing spikes strategically placed throughout the tread to protect my head, limbs and vital organs. Armed and ready, God began sending me out on short missions. God had specially selected business and film agents for me to work with, and quickly I became known as a trouble shooter. Because of my faithfulness in helping others with their businesses, God has given me a colossal project of my own; a multimedia corporate structure that involves technology that does not yet exist.

In 2007, God told me that my company is to expand worldwide. One pastor prophesied that God had given me a plan to save the world, just like He did Joseph in the Bible. Yes God gave me a plan, but just like Joseph, my brothers in the faith threatened my life, put me in a pit and sold me into slavery. This is no exaggeration. They attempted to sell me into sex trafficking. God had warned me that this was going to happen, then men started showing up. One man said that he *"paid good money"* for me, and that I *"owed"* him. He even had the nerve to say that he *"owned"* me. Instead of being scared, I became angry. He had a lot of nerve. This man had no idea who he was speaking to. I blasted that man by telling, that I was bought with the Blood of Jesus; that God owned me, and if he was going to pursue after me trying to get what he thought he was owed, he had just set himself up for a battle with Almighty God. Fortunately this altercation happened in public. There had to be at least forty-fifty witnesses, who actually stopped and began cheering for me. That fool thought he could scare me. I met up with the wrong one that day. A Holy Ghost boldness had taken over me. Never again will a let a man, or anyone bully me, in Jesus' Name!

What the enemy meant for evil, God turned into my good! Supernatural things began happening all around me. It was apparent that my natural gifts in music, technology and writing were never meant just to entertain or enlighten audiences. I see the supernatural in operation, bring healing, deliverance, and believe it or not money and prosperity wherever I go. It's not me. It's the God in me, moving on the inside and manifesting on the outside in ways I have never known. A great transformation has occurred in me. It's still me, but even better than I could ever be on my own.

God demonstrated in the most unusual ways that my gifts belong to him to use as he pleases. Now, there is a strong prophetic influence on everything that I do. All of my natural gifts operate supernaturally whenever God wills. The most surprising, is my prophetic speech. I will speak what Heaven speaks and it bypasses my mind. Words will come out of my mouth that I have never heard before; and with it comes an anointing (power) that changes circumstances instantly. I know for a fact, that I have been supernaturally endowed by God to do mighty works in this world!

In Pursuit Of Super Heroic Enduring Faith

In the Kingdom, when we obey God, *his supernatural laws supersede every law in the universe*, even man-made laws. When obey Him we invoke the Finger of God to do the work through us. It is then that the Kingdom of God and His power will take over the situation. That which is impossible for men becomes possible for God; because with God, all things are possible.

The Finger of God is mentioned in the Bible as it relates to miracles that were publicly performed and criticized.[xliii] When Jesus cast a devil out and the naysayers said that he cast out demons with the power of the devil. Jesus told them that if He cast out the devil with the Finger of God then this was evidence that the Kingdom of God was operating in their midst. When Moses obeyed God and caused plagues to come upon Egypt. Pharaoh just assumed that his magicians could do the same, until they explained that this was not magic, but the Finger of God operating against Pharaoh.

When you began operating in the supernatural power of God, some will say it is magic or the power of Satan. This is normal. Do not be alarmed when they attack you. Let them talk. They only harm themselves. Jesus said that we are blessed when men say all manner of evil against us falsely for his name's sake. We are to rejoice and leap for joy![xliv] For great is our reward in Heaven. It may hurt to see people you love turn against you, but obey God anyway. It takes great faith to follow God. It also takes great courage and endurance to keep the faith in the midst of adversity. One must always remember that the Greater One is inside of the believer. There is nothing impossible to overcome. We will have what God promised if we refuse to give up.

I am reminded of something I heard while going through my transformation. It was about 3 am when I was awaken by these words speaking in my spirit. ***"As kids, we played, Let's Pretend; what we will have or what we will be. But this life in Christ, we don't have to pretend. We can have what God says, if we don't faint due to pain, sickness and unbelief. If we don't receive, it's because we never really believed."*** This is faith in a nutshell. We have to continue to believe what God says no matter what. If we don't, then we never really had faith to begin with. Faith is certain. Faith is bold and reassured. Once you have heard from God directly, you have what is necessary to go forth in faith. You're not taking the word of someone else. You're not just hoping something would happen. *You have heard from God directly*. To doubt God is to call him a liar. God cannot lie. He is not like us.[xlv] His word will come to pass, if not for us, it will come to pass for someone else who stands in faith.

You would be Superheroes Of The Cross, what are you waiting on? Not enough money, time or education? Ask God where to begin and just step out on faith. What you lack will be provided. If you wait until you have enough of what you think you need, it will never happen for you. God knows what you lack. God wants us to come in faith, just as we are. People may say, "No one can do that." And they would be right. Impossible situations are God's speciality. This is how God operates in this earth. God just needs someone willing and obedient who believes Him. The the supernatural power of the Holy Ghost can quicken us and turn us into super heroic beings; doing mighty feats in the earth to the glory of God the Father!

CONCLUSION

The Superhero's Kryptonite

Comic fans know that every superhero has a weakness that must be avoided if they want to keep their powers at peak performance. We've all heard of Superman's kryptonite. As the story goes, there are many forms of kryptonite, but the one that the enemy uses in the popular stories, is the green kryptonite that weakness and sickens the hero. Likewise, there is something used against the Superheroes Of The Cross that is analogous to kryptonite, it's called the *human flesh; which encompasses the human mind, will, emotions and intellect.* We alluded to this weakness in an earlier chapter, but now we will discuss why it is vital to avoid operating in the flesh. It has to do with the *motivations of one's heart.*

We've discussed how the Word of God is essential to every Superhero in the Kingdom. It is a discerner of the thoughts and motives of one's heart.[xlvi] Everyone desiring to be a Superhero must be skillful in using the Word of God; or else they run the risk of getting hurt while wielding that lightening swift sword at the enemy. The Word of God has no favorites. No one can get away with violating God's word. Even God cannot violate the word that He has spoken. It doesn't matter who you are. If you violate the word, and you don't repent, you will have to pay a penalty. The Kingdom of God is ruled by righteousness. It is the way God and His Kingdom operates. The Kingdom also operates by the *royal law of love.* Faith works by love.[xlvii] It cannot work when one walks in the flesh. You can do all the right things with the wrong motive, and it will count against you. The flesh lusts against the spirit, and leads to sin and corruption. Moses was God's hero who delivered the Children of Israel out of slavery in Egypt. His assignment was to take them in the promised land. Moses saw the promise, but was not allowed to go in with God's people. Moses let his anger takeover and he lost his position. God ordered him to die.[xlviii] King Solomon was another of God's heroes. He was the wisest and richest king who ever lived. Solomon had seven hundred wives and three hundred concubines, who turn his heart against God.[xlix] The Lord said he was going to strip the kingdom from Solomon, but because of His vow to his father David, God split the kingdom. He gave ten of the twelve tribes to Solomon's servant. The remainder went to Solomon's son. A rivalry arose between the kingdoms, that would last for generations to come.

There is a misconception among Christians. Some believe that if God uses you mightily, you are somehow exempt from paying penalties for sins of the flesh. In God's Kingdom, the wages (penalty) of sin is death.[1] Jesus died so that we may be free of this penalty, but a person who receives Jesus' payment and then continues to sin reneges on the deal. The exchange is no longer valid. John 3:16 says, *For God so loved the world that he gave his only gotten son; that whoever believes in him SHOULD NOT perish, but have everlasting life.* This means that God gives us an opportunity so that we might not perish. He will not change his mind, but it is not uncommon for people to change their mind and turn from God when things get tough. If they do not turn back and repent, they will die in their sin.

This is why is it important to follow after God and His word and not compare ourselves to others. We cannot always tell who is with or against God. The wheat and the tare are allowed to grow up in the Kingdom together. We need to weight our accomplishments based upon the Word of God and what God has spoken directly to our spirit. Integrity in God's word is required of superheroes. We walk by faith and not by sight. A Superhero can be easily fooled if he or she is operating by their physical senses. Our battles are spiritual in nature. We discern truth by the spirit, not by what we have seen or heard. There are well meaning people that have not heard from God concerning you. Don't even take their word over what God has told you. Then there are the pretenders (the tare) they sound like they know what is going on, but they are the false prophets and counterfeit believers; wolves in sheep's clothing. Here is an example of how important it is to obey God's word regardless of who tells you to do otherwise. The story can be found in I Kings Chapter 13. This is one of those Bible stories that I never liked nor understood, until the Lord explained it to me.

God sends a young prophet with a specific word to deliver to a King. This was the last chance for this king to repent for the sake of God's people. God gave this young prophet **specific instructions** saying, *"Don't go home with anyone, nor eat or drink with them, and don't go back home the same way you came."* The young prophet delivered the message. The king was happy that he was being restored to God, and offered to thank the prophet with food and drink. The young prophet told the king that God would not let him eat or drink with anyone. He went on his way. Then, there was an old prophet who heard about what the young prophet had done, and he sent men to invite the young prophet to stay and eat with them. The young prophet said that God forbid him to do such, but the old prophet insisted that he had also heard from God. The old prophet told the young prophet that God said it was okay for them to spend time together. The older prophet had lied. He never heard from God at all. So, the young prophet, not knowing he had been deceived, visited with the old prophet. While they were eating, God used the mouth of the lying old prophet to curse the young prophet. From the mouth of the old prophet, God said that the young prophet would die that day. On his way home the young prophet was killed by a lion and never made it home.

When the younger prophet yielded to the authority of the elder prophet, rather than obeying God; he honored the old prophet and dishonored God. The fact that the old prophet lied did not matter to God because the young prophet was given specific instructions that he was told to follow no matter what.

Even though the young prophet's death was a sad event, what followed was even worse. As the story ends, the king heard about the young prophet's death, and no longer desired to repent. The king turned from God and was destroyed from the face of the earth. He too had invited the young prophet to eat with him. The young prophet said he could not because of God's instruction, but yet he disobeyed those same instructions in order to eat with the older prophet. It was the young prophet's hypocrisy that caused the king to sin against God.

No matter what comes your way, remember that Superheroes are empowered to do good works so that the world would desire our God. His Word is Law. Obey God. If problems arise, go to God and let him further instruct you. At the end of the day you want him to say, *"Well done my good and faithful servant."*

So You Want To Be A Superhero

You've heard what's required. You've read one superhero's testimony, and now you want to be transformed and step into you new supernatural life. Remember, every Superhero has an archenemy who will continually try to overthrow your powers, but this is your fight of faith. Fight through your own self-doubts and the doubts of others around you. Keep the faith. After all, your superhero status and assignment were designed specifically for you by God. It's His Spirit that will transform your spirit. It's His Word that will renew your mind. Where the mind goes, the body will follow.

You can do all things through Christ (the anointed one and his anointing) who strengthens you. It's not by your might but by God's Spirit that you succeed in all things. Get rid of sin. It will hinder the Word of God. Sin is a hindrance and weight you do not need. A superhero needs all his strength in order to be successful. If you handicap yourself with sin, you will only do your archenemy a favor. He doesn't have to kill you. He will watch you commit suicide with own sinful acts.

The greatest superhero to ever live was Jesus. Use him as your example. He only did and said what God told him to do and say. Jesus was tempted by the devil, but never sinned. He obeyed the commandments of God even to death on the cross. Jesus said that if any man wanted to follow his example, then deny yourself (the lust, the sin, the selfish desires), pick up your cross (this is the challenge that you must overcome in order to obey God), and follow him.[li] It's not an easy road, and the path is narrow.[lii] In fact, few people can even find it. But we have shown you the way. If you are ready, and then follow the instructions that follow.

We start with the cross (your superhero phone booth) and transform you from darkness to light; from the power of satan to the power of God. Then you can begin on your journey to receive your inheritance and the blessings that are waiting for you. Just pray this prayer out loud.

Dear God in Heaven,
I am sorry that I have sinned against you by doing my own thing. I want your plan and purpose to manifest in my life. Thank you for sending your son Jesus to earth. I accept his payment for my sins. I want Jesus to be Lord over my life. I renounce sin and all satanic holds on my life. Fill me with your Holy Spirit, and let your resurrection power fill my entire being. Holy Spirit, lead me each day, to God's purpose for my life. Father, thank you for loving me and allowing me another chance at life; not just any life, but the abundant life that only your kingdom can provide. I believe in my heart and confess with my mouth that I have received all that I have asked for this day, in Jesus' Name. Amen.

If you prayed this prayer, welcome to the family of God! Find a good Bible teaching church in your area. Start praying (talking) to God and reading your Bible daily. It's the fuel you will need to sustain your faith each day. Stay tuned to the Holy Spirit and ask him to show you God's plan for your life. He will also teach you the mysteries of the Bible and show you things concerning your life. Make him your best friend and you will experience the supernatural power of God in ways that will significantly enhance your life. Enjoy your new family. Walk obedience to the Holy Spirit, and watch the power of God's Kingdom manifest before your very eyes!

Faith's Superheroes

And What Shall I More Say?

For the time would fail me to tell of Gedeon, and of Barak, and of Samson,
and of Jephthae;
of David also,
and Samuel, and of the prophets:

Who Through Faith

Subdued Kingdoms,
Wrought Righteousness,
Obtained Promises,
Stopped The Mouths Of Lions,
Quenched the violence of fire,
Escaped The Edge Of The Sword,
Out Of Weakness
Were Made Strong,
Waxed Valiant In Fight,
Turned To Flight
The Armies Of The Aliens.

Hebrews 11:32-34

But
Seek Ye First
The Kingdom Of God,
And His Righteousness;
And
All These Things
Shall Be Added Unto You.

Matthew 6:33

MORE FROM THE AUTHOR

Paula Matthews is an author and speaker whose prophetic writings have captured the attention of many enthusiastic followers after the initial release of *The War Journal (1999-2010) Volume I* in 2010. The book spawned dozens of online discussions.

Additionally, Ms. Matthews has been sharing her prophetic life lessons as an Expert Author for EzineArticles.com.

Additional Titles
Available in Print and eBook Formats

The War Journal (1999-2010) Volume I
The Visions, Dreams And Prophecies From Almighty God
Concerning War IN America

The War Journal (1999-2010) Volume II
The Seat Of War: The Christian Church In America
The War Stories And Their Meaning

EPIC Books And Café Presents Book Discussion
Of The War Journal (1999-2010) Volume I

ENDNOTES

i   I Samuel 17:41-51; 16:1-13
ii   Daniel 6:1-28
iii   Daniel 3:1-30
iv   Luke 9:38-44
v   Luke 7:22
vi   Matthew 14:13-21; 17:27; Mark 6:31-44; Luke 9:12-17; John 6:1-14
vii   James 5:17-18
viii   Joshua 10:12-13
ix   Joshua 6:20
x   II Chronicles 16:9; John 3:16
xi   John 14:6
xii   Matthew 7:14
xiii   Genesis 2:15
xiv   Psalm 2:8; Luke 22:29
xv   Revelation 1:6; 5:1; I Peter 2:9
xvi   Ephesians 1:14
xvii   I John 4:17
xviii   Ephesians 1:3-4, 20; 2:4-7
xix   John 1:12-13
xx   II Peter 1:4
xxi   John 14:26
xxii   Hebrews 4:12
xxiii   Psalm 119:105
xxiv   Isaiah 55:11
xxv   John 6:63
xxvi   I Thessalonians 1:9
xxvii   Psalm 82:6
xxviii   John 3:34
xxix   Exodus 7:1
xxx   Acts 17:26
xxxi   II Corinthians 12:9-10
xxxii   I Corinthians 1:27-28
xxxiii   John 14:10
xxxiv   Ephesians 3:16; Philippians 4:13
xxxv   Romans 12:3
xxxvi   Ephesians 6:12
xxxvii   I Peter 5:8

ENDNOTES *(CONTINUED)*

xxxviii Luke 10:19
xxxix   Matthew 28:18; Hebrews 2:8
xl   Psalm 105:15
xli   Deuteronomy 28:7
xlii   Isaiah 40:31
xliii   Exodus 8:19; Luke 11:20
xliv   Matthew 5:10-12; Luke 6:22-23
xlv   Numbers 23:19
xlvi   Hebrews 4:12
xlvii   Galatians 5:6
xlviii Numbers 20:7-13; Deuteronomy 32:48-52
xlix   I Kings 11:1-43
l   Romans 6:23
li   Matthew 16:24
lii   Matthew 7:14

www.ingramcontent.com/pod-product-compliance
Lightning Source LLC
Chambersburg PA
CBHW060053050426
42448CB00011B/2441